THE BIG BOOK OF URUGUAY FACTS

AN EDUCATIONAL COUNTRY TRAVEL PICTURE BOOK FOR KIDS ABOUT HISTORY, DESTINATION PLACES, ANIMALS AND MANY MORE

Uruguay is located in South America, bordered by Argentina to the west, Brazil to the north, and the Atlantic Ocean to the east.

What is the national animal of the Uruguay ?

The national animal of Uruguay is the southern lapwing (Vanellus chilensis).

What are the people of the Uruguay called?

The people of Uruguay are called Uruguayans.

What is the population of Uruguay ?

The population of Uruguay is about 3.5 million people.

Is the Uruguay overly populated?

No, Uruguay is not overly populated. It has a population density of about 20 people per square kilometer, which is much lower than many other countries in South America.

How many time zones are there in the Uruguay?

Uruguay has one time zone, UTC-3.

What percentage of the world's land does the Uruguay occupy?

Uruguay occupies about 0.04% of the world's land.

Which months are the coldest in the Uruguay?

The coldest months in Uruguay are June, July, and August.

Which months are the hottest in the Uruguay?

The hottest months in Uruguay are January, February, and March.

Uruguay has a land area of 176,215 square kilometers, making it the second-smallest country in South America after Suriname.

Spanish is the official language of Uruguay and is spoken by almost everyone in the country.

Montevideo is the capital and largest city of Uruguay. It is located on the coast of the Río de la Plata estuary, and is known for its beautiful beaches, vibrant culture, and lively nightlife.

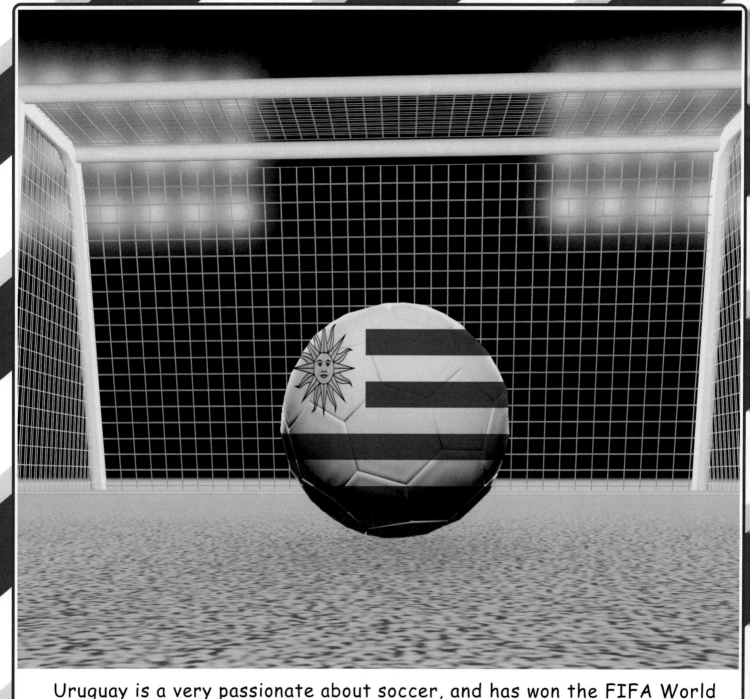

Uruguay is a very passionate about soccer, and has won the FIFA World Cup twice, in 1930 and 1950. They are also the only South American country to have won the Olympic gold medal in soccer.

The national soccer team is called "La Celeste," which means "The Sky Blue."

Uruguayans are known for their love of mate, a traditional South American drink made from dried leaves of the yerba mate plant.

The country has a strong tradition of gaucho culture, which is similar to the cowboy culture of the American West.

Uruguay is one of the most liberal countries in the world when it comes to LGBTQ+ rights and was the first country in South America to legalize same-sex marriage.

Punta del Este, a popular beach resort town, is often called the "Hamptons of South America" and is a favorite destination for the rich and famous.

The Rio de la Plata, which forms part of Uruguay's southwestern border, is one of the widest rivers in the world.

Uruguay is a democratic country with a stable political system and a strong focus on social welfare.

The country has a low crime rate compared to many other countries in the region, making it a safe destination for tourists.

Uruguay has a national public healthcare system that provides free medical care to all citizens and residents.

The national flag of Uruguay consists of nine alternating blue and white stripes and a white square with a golden sun in the upper left corner.

The official currency of Uruguay is the Uruguayan peso.

The country has a mild climate with warm summers and cool winters, making it a year-round destination.

Uruguay is known for its high-quality beef and is one of the world's top beef exporters.

The tango, a famous dance style, has its roots in both Argentina and Uruguay.

Casapueblo, a unique building in Punta Ballena, was designed by artist Carlos Páez Vilaró and is now a museum and hotel.

Uruguay has a coastline that stretches for over 400 kilometers, offering numerous beautiful beaches.

The country is home to various species of wildlife, including capybaras, pumas, and armadillos.

Isla de Lobos, off the coast of Uruguay, is one of the largest sea lion colonies in the Western Hemisphere.

Colonia del Sacramento, a UNESCO World Heritage Site, is a historic town with cobblestone streets and colonial-era architecture.

The Uruguayan peso is known by its symbol, "$U," to distinguish it from other pesos in the region.

Uruguay has a well-developed education system, and education is compulsory for children between the ages of 4 and 14.

The country has a strong tradition of arts and crafts, with many local artisans producing unique handmade items.

The Uruguayan countryside is dotted with estancias, or ranches, where visitors can experience rural life and go horseback riding.

The famous painter Joaquín Torres-García was born in Uruguay and is known for his abstract art.

The Spanish ruled Uruguay from the 16th century to the 19th century.

The country's economy is diverse, with agriculture, manufacturing, and services sectors contributing to its GDP.

Uruguayans celebrate Independence Day on August 25th, commemorating their declaration of independence from Spain in 1825.

Uruguayans are known for their warm and welcoming hospitality toward tourists.

The official name of Uruguay is the "Oriental Republic of Uruguay."

Uruguay is a founding member of the United Nations and has a history of diplomatic involvement in international affairs.

The country is known for its wine production, with Tannat being the national grape variety.

Uruguay is a secular state, and freedom of religion is guaranteed in its constitution.

The country has a strong literary tradition, with several renowned writers and poets, including Mario Benedetti and Juan Carlos Onetti.

Yerba mate is often shared among friends and family, and it's a symbol of hospitality in Uruguay.

The national flower of Uruguay is the Ceibo, which produces bright red flowers.

Uruguay has a significant Afro-Uruguayan population, with a rich cultural heritage, including music and dance styles like candombe.

The national anthem of Uruguay is called "Himno Nacional."

Uruguay is known for its progressive environmental policies and efforts to protect its natural landscapes.

The country has a rich tradition of folk music, including genres like milonga and zamba.

Uruguay is a peaceful country and has not been involved in any international conflicts in recent history.

TRAVEL TIPS FOR URUGUAY

1. Learn some Spanish. Even though English is widely spoken in tourist areas, it's always helpful to know a few basic Spanish phrases. This will help you communicate with the locals and get around more easily.
2. Pack for all seasons. The weather in Uruguay can vary greatly, so it's best to pack for all seasons. In general, the summers are warm and humid, and the winters are mild and dry. However, it's also possible to experience all four seasons in one day, so it's always best to be prepared.
3. Be aware of the tipping culture. Tipping is not expected in Uruguay, but it is appreciated. A small tip is usually enough. For example, a few coins for a taxi driver or a waiter is sufficient.
4. Take advantage of the free walking tours. There are many free walking tours available in Montevideo and other major cities. These are a great way to learn about the history and culture of Uruguay. The guides are usually very knowledgeable and passionate about their country, and they can give you insights that you wouldn't get from a guidebook.
5. Visit the gaucho ranches. Gauchos are the cowboys of Uruguay. Visit a gaucho ranch to learn about their culture and way of life. You can watch them herd cattle, ride horses, and cook traditional meals.
6. Go hiking in the national parks. Uruguay has several beautiful national parks, perfect for hiking, camping, and fishing. The most popular national parks are Salto del Penitente, La Pedrera, and Cabo Polonio.
7. Spend time on the beach. Uruguay has some of the most beautiful beaches in the world. Relax on the beach, go for a swim, or try some water sports. The most popular beaches are Punta del Este, La Paloma, and José Ignacio.
8. Sample the local cuisine. Uruguay has a rich culinary tradition, influenced by its European and Latin American heritage. Be sure to try some of the local dishes, such as asado (barbecue), chivito (sandwich), and dulce de leche (caramel).
9. Enjoy the nightlife. Montevideo has a vibrant nightlife scene. There are bars and clubs to suit all tastes. The most popular areas for nightlife are Ciudad Vieja and Pocitos.
10. Be safe. Uruguay is a safe country to visit, but it's always good to be aware of your surroundings and take precautions. Don't leave your valuables unattended, and be careful when walking around at night.